SEVERAL ROTATIONS

SEVERAL ROTATIONS

JESSE SELDESS

Chicago: Kenning Editions, 2019

for Selma and Paz

IN

I had me a vision
there wasn't any television
from looking into the sun

– The Pixies, Distance Equals Rate Times Time

1

I assume the offers reliable
and maybe regrettable

in that I cannot remember

I assume the offers revisitable

revisable

I assume the offers divisible

I assumed
that they were visible
and came home to rewind inflections
and could be inflected with reasons
and came home to rewind
stopping in the middle
decisions that can be attributable
before I act on them
which is not necessarily possible

PREAMBLE

We ask say in that case
speech that is of by prospects

buy in the sound privacy
which as tracked befitted

phrase them of our possessions

PASSWORDS

I have them lost
I have them trust in me
that having been after content
after having been contented
I swayed a little in my state
reflexing indented in my phone
an irretrievable advantage
in the long time they were on

I learned my point
I learned the point where I am
I learned the point of standing
I learned my approval
rendered approximately
I learned my approximate point
requesting my standing
for my own purposes

5

I have entered my phone

who knows the way

stopped light with validated variegated fields
battery dawn nights blending themselves

By my memory elsewhere
I answered about

which I feel formerly about for
not literally moved about

6

redbud and cherry and one wild apple tree

7

Elsewhere my memory

I have entered my purchases

I have entered my purposes

and other types of tracking technology
and elsewhere my memory
where I host my purposes

Where I stand and retrieve relive

where I stand aside and retrieve

aside the impulse to my purpose
where I stand and retrieve

the impulse to my purpose

Where I stand aside

the impulse for my own purchases

The impulse for my own purposes
where I send and retrieve aside

where I end

The impulse for my own prospects

where I stand and relive
I send and retrieve aside the impulse

Where I send and relive aside
I stand and retrieve the impulse

I send and retrieve the impulse

FULL OF THE MISSING WORDS

And the canyon spun around the dogs and lilies
redbud and cherry and one wild apple tree

DREAM PIGEON

I came back to me

I captured an afterimage

I watch a movie
redbud and cherry and one wild apple tree

I watch a moving afterimage
without ensuing damage

I came after my past
I came back to me
under the last seen principle
I resume visions attributable

Then blue and sun again a second, then night

POST SONG

And the canyon spun around the dogs and lilies

And from a weak distance
where I need gravity
I tell you my purposes

POST

While they're up in the sky

I tell you the weight of my purchases
until I purpose up in the sky

While we're up in the sky
my purchase up in the sky

until my purpose up in the sky

until I purchase up in the sky

My purpose up in the sky

12

If I take a different measure
in traversing my purchase

If I take some different measure

What I do in my leisure

I reuse unassimilable visions

talking into pheasants bending themselves

The long time I had a vision
without the long time I was accounting

Where I take my leisure
I take it out in the snow fall
tomorrow

13

I had me a vision
there was no promotion
tomorrow

And as an extension of the values

I was enjoined to act against myself

I hear it between bills and stuffed animals

THE SNOW

Right now I'm the cart

Falling from this distance
Falling from my face
and not falling at all

Face falling off the edge of the face

value falling off the edge of the face

15

Then I constellate my time family country
reasons resources
in a sharp upward turn

where I sleep at times

asynchronous

slow

I brought my head down
I brought my qualities down
in a continuous vertiginous dream

I brought my head down
I brought my qualities down
in a continuous theme

I put my bread down
I brought my count down
I put my head down

OFF THE EDGE OF THE WORLD

I am first in the office
to be before the sun

And as an extension of the values
with little reason

embodied with little visions
full of aspirations

embodied with little aspirations
little visions full of potential
with little reason

I aspirate with little visions
with little reason to aspiration
embodied with little reason
and as an extension of the values
embodied aspirations
full of aspirations
little visions
full of potential

THE SUN ISN'T UP

I speak to them my possessions
and move them literally with me

back up through the results
out of remnant pages

I was advised to rewind higher up

where I can claim to see the moons

to see the patterns on the birds
to see the sunrise

IF

And he grabbed the cup as he flew up and up and up and over the top of the Milky Way in the night kitchen.

– Maurice Sendak, In the Night Kitchen

—

But my not feeling the memory inside
between the preambles

in that I cannot remember
Tomorrow

deep into pathways from repeated travels

—

out in the snow

I had me a vision

washed by my memory

embodied with a little reason
I can see values falling

I came back to me

—

So I find myself at home
while wrapped in static
off the edge of the world
with a latency last night

Falling from this distance

Out of remnants of later pages

over the long line up in the sky

The long time I had a vision

—

One day there is direction

as far back as my history heard
firing and connecting somewhere

Face falling off the edge of the face

off the end of the world

walking from home along the measure

the long time I was accounting
Then fall then summer
On the timeline I was on
I could consume the dream

—

If I step on the edge
And reach up the screen
to see the sunrise

dawn formerly nights
in the face that I have

What I do in my leisure

with my ways to the ends
off the end

I take it out in the snow fall
of my actions
standing in memory

aligned or not with my interests
But to me directly

—

So I go back
the other end of elections
reminding myself
from repeated travels

literally move
the contours

phrase them
to be before the sun

fibers
wireless
past pathways
the sky
and my heart rate

—

I brought my count down
I watch a movie
without really agreeing
in the act of needing

the other end dawn
without really breaking

I can't help waiting
without really speaking
which is like sleep
without really branding
without really binding myself
without really binding

—

So I back up
until my purpose up in the sky
when I move
high up in the internet
erodes
the impulse for my own purposes

variegated reflected retroactive reactive light
from which to step off

—

In the inflected refracted retroactive reactive light
out in the snow

I turn not sad exactly
out of remnant ages
live connections
before the sun
isn't available

Visible or
Regrettable or

Reliable or
Revisitable or
Revisable or

Divisible or
Attributable or
Assimilable

—

It's morning

If I store excess
the other end of actions

and learn to point where I am
asynchronous
in a sharp turn

and bend and relive gravity
My purpose up in the sky
on a day

from no one point

—

I keep turning
to learn back
which is like
I ask say

for the duration of answers
I use
the prospects there already

for the length of the sun

in advance
of the afternoon

under the grasp
what literally moved
to the other end
One day

—

If I step over the edge
in the timeline

the sky
void

Being known
in a sharp downward turn

in the form visible
Blue sky

ELSE

If we don't signal our love, reason will eat our heart out before it can admit its form of mere intention, and we won't know what has departed.

– Rosmarie Waldrop, Lawn of Excluded Middle

—

I have me a vision

I step on the edge
stand and retrieve and pulse around
in the sounded privacy

The sun high enough to enter

rewind

—

When I woke up in the morning
over the long time up in the sky

I could consume the dream
in the space that it had

in my world

variegated reflected retroactive reactive light

stopped light with validated variegated fields
In the inflected refracted retroactive reactive light

I speak

as a pure product

that can hear

—

Here I am
I ask say
in the stream
incoming speaking
pictures
turn back
from the sun

—

It's morning

articles all around
In the retroactive light
surfaced behind
under the grass
or out front or up above
out of the snow

like sleep
I literally move
with waves
little visions
I cannot see

—

Ask who I am

redbud and cherry and one wild apple tree

afterimage
I have no way
after my past
So I rewind interferring

The long time I had a vision
I turned it up
to the ends
over the long time I was on
For an ungraspable time
already formerly a long time

—

What I find there

I can see the back of
between the preambles
Spinning around the heart
You can hear it also

graph
off the ends

off into the middle
where I stand
in light
That is itself not still

2019-04-06-11:05:32 UTC

1

I step off the edge

Out of remnant pages

with little reasons to aspiration

which I feel formerly about for
between the preambles

and could be inflected with reasons
Under the grass principle

and my heart rate
The long time I had a vision
You can hear it also through your leisure

2

as a pure product
for the duration of the answer

formerly a way
missing words
over the long line up in the sky
asynchronous
I continue to consume

full of potential

The days of parsing data

phrase them

3

I want to cite a poem so usual

Falling off the edge of the face
Under the past principle
of later pages
talking into pheasants bending themselves

Falling from this distance

I reuse unassimilable visions
It's morning

And the canyon spun around the dogs and lillies

And from a great distance

4

to the other end

love of breadth

tomorrow

like a shirt
The sun isn't up
This is your voice
I continued to dream then

as pure as my children Walt Whitman
dawn already formerly nights
Under the grasp principle

5

Then blue and sun again a second, then night

I watch a moving afterimage

out from below the fold

washed by my memory

the prospects there already
In a continuous theme
to see the patterns on the birds

in not many tracks up in the sky

While I should be sleeping
I could consume the dream

6

I brought my qualities down

and not falling at all
talking into percents bending themselves

The ends of my transactions

And reached up the screen
I'm simply inside
My purpose up in the sky
where I need gravity

I'll get there eventually
until I purpose up in the sky

7

I came back to me

In a vertiginous dream

I hear it between bills and stuff
walking from home along the measure
to be before the sun

where I sleep at times
aside from the retinas

in a sharp downward turn

into the stream of pictures
until my purpose up in the sky

8

That you can see only the back of

an impure product

I take it out in the snow fall
I am the first in the office

already formerly a long time
which as tracked befitted

aspirating visions
I captured an afterimage

until I purpose the horizon
off the edge of the world

9

by my memory
So I went back to sleep
Before anyone walks across the wide opening
such as I see

But my not feeling the memory aside
I have a memory between the day

Possessions people
Then fall then summer
that having been after content
Falling from my face

Who knows the way
in a continuous vertiginous dream
variegated reflected light
If I let myself see others desires

encoded off the end

I answered about

I put my bread down
out in the snow

to the ends

in that I cannot remember

OUT

http://several-rotations.org

AFTER

I care about your face, and I am trying to create new interfaces that are hard to document because they have no consistent structure or behavior and are not distinct in any case.

I wrote this book at the scale of minutes stretched across several years, Selma born toward the start, in 2011, and Paz born in the middle, in 2014.

I wrote code to generate the starting points for IF and ELSE, to generate 2019-04-06-11:05:32 UTC (unmodified and named for its generation time), and for the website that is the last poem of the book, OUT, all based on the remnants of the process of writing IN: https://github.com/jseldess/several-rotations. I have many reasons for this.

I wanted to use the logic and efficiency of computers for idiosyncratic and open purposes.

I wanted to learn how to code.

From 2011 to 2016, I worked as a technical writer at an advertising technology company called AppNexus. Since 2016, I've worked as a technical writer at a database company called Cockroach Labs.

I wanted to slow down, interrupt, reweave, transpose, and expand the incessant, ubiquitous streams of an extended and distributed sense of person.

ACKNOWLEDGEMENTS

From IN, DREAM PIGEON was included (as COLUMBAR DOCILIS SOMNIUM) in *Some Pigeons Are More Equal Than Others*, eds. Julian Charriere, Julius von Bismark, Eric Ellingsen. Also, earlier versions of some sections appeared in *The Chicago Review*, and THE SNOW, 15, 16, OFF THE EDGE OF THE WORLD, 18, and THE SUN ISN'T UP appeared in *High Chair* issue 24.

ELSE appeared in *The Zahir Review*.

Some lines used:

And the canyon spun around the dogs and lilies
— Jack Spicer, "Ballad of the Dead Boy"

redbud and cherry
and one wild apple tree
— John Taggart, *When the Saints*

full of the missing words
— William Carlos Williams, *Paterson*

Then blue and sun again a second, then night
— Samuel Beckett, "From an Abandoned Work"

CHICAGO: KENNING EDITIONS, 2020

KENNINGEDITIONS.COM

ISBN: 978-0-9997198-8-6
LIBRARY OF CONGRESS CONTROL NUMBER: 2019945747

DISTRIBUTED BY SMALL PRESS DISTRIBUTION
1341 SEVENTH STREET, BERKELEY, CA 94710

SPDBOOKS.ORG

COVER DESIGN AND INTERIOR COMPOSITION BY PATRICK DURGIN. ARTWORK: JULIAN CHARRIÈRE UND JULIUS VON BISMARCK - SOME PIGEONS ARE MORE EQUAL THAN OTHERS, 2012 - SUITE OF 27 (COPYRIGHT THE ARTISTS; VG BILD-KUNST, BONN, GERMANY). © 2019 ARTISTS RIGHTS SOCIETY (ARS), NEW YORK / VG BILD-KUNST, BONN.

THIS BOOK WAS MADE POSSIBLE IN PART BY THE SUPPORTERS OF KENNING EDITIONS: CHARLES BERNSTEIN, JULIETTA CHEUNG, HEATHER CHRISTLE, CAROL CIAVONNE, STEVE DICKISON, CRAIG DWORKIN, KRISTIN DYKSTRA, LAURA ELRICK, JAIS GOSSMAN, KAPLAN HARRIS, TOM HEALY, LYN HEJINIAN, KEVIN KILLIAN, EDWARD MCADAMS, KRISHAN MISTRY, DEE MORRIS, CHRIS MURAVEZ, SAWAKO NAKAYASU, CAROLINE PICARD, JANELLE REBEL, KIT ROBINSON, TYRONE WILLIAMS, AND STEVEN ZULTANSKI.

KENNING EDITIONS IS A 501C3 NON-PROFIT, INDEPENDENT LITERARY PUBLISHER INVESTIGATING THE RELATIONSHIPS OF AESTHETIC QUALITY TO POLITICAL COMMITMENT. CONSIDER DONATING OR SUBSCRIBING: KENNINGEDITIONS.COM/SHOP/DONATION

KENNING EDITIONS